CW01333408

Text: Keith Fergus
Series editor: Tony Bowerman
Photographs: Keith Fergus/ www.scottishhorizons.photoshelter.com, Laura Hodgkinson, Alamy, Shutterstock, Dreamstime
Design: Carl Rogers and Laura Hodgkinson

© Northern Eye Books Limited 2018
Keith Fergus has asserted his rights under the Copyright, Designs and Patents Act, 1988 to be identified as the author of this work. All rights reserved.

This book contains mapping data licensed from the Ordnance Survey with the permission of the Controller of Her Majesty's Stationery Office. © Crown copyright 2018. All rights reserved. Licence number 100047867

Northern Eye Books

ISBN 978-1-908632-56-2

A CIP catalogue record for this book is available from the British Library.

www.northerneyebooks.co.uk

Cover: Ben Arthur/The Cobbler (Walk 3)

Warning!

Walking and scrambling in the mountains can be dangerous and carries the risk of personal injury or death. Do not attempt these walks unless you have suitable experience or training. Conditions can change rapidly, particularly on high ground, and it is important that walkers have the ability to assess both the conditions and the associated risks.

Important Advice: The routes described in this book are undertaken at the readers own risk. Walkers should take into account their level of fitness, wear suitable footwear and clothing, and carry food and water**. It is also advisable to take the relevant OS map with you in case you get lost or leave the area covered by our maps.**

Whilst every care has been taken to ensure the accuracy of the route directions, the publishers cannot accept responsibility for errors or omissions, or for changes in the details given. Nor can the publisher and copyright owners accept responsibility for any consequences arising from the use of this book.

If you find any inaccuracies in either the text or maps, please write to us or email us at the address below. Thank you.

First published in 2018 by
Northern Eye Books Limited

Northern Eye Books, Tattenhall, Cheshire CH3 9PX

tony@northerneyebooks.com

www.northerneyebooks.co.uk

@northerneyebooks

@northerneyeboo

For sales enquiries, please call 01928 723 744

Contents

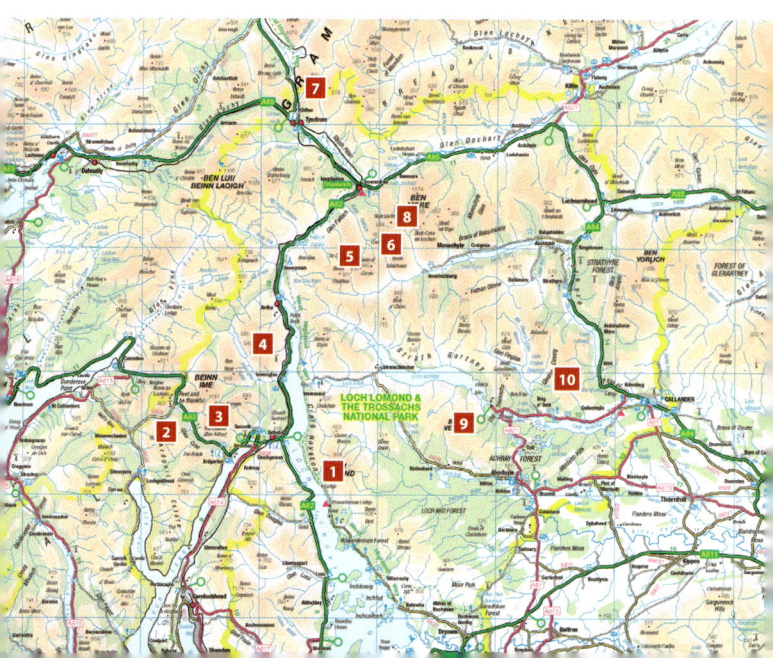

Scotland's First National Park 4

Top 10 Walks: Easy Summits 6

1 | **Ben Lomond** (Ptarmigan Ridge) .. 8

2 | **Ben Donich** 14

3 | **The Cobbler** 20

4 | **Ben Vorlich** 26

5 | **An Caisteal** 30

6 | **Cruach Ardrain** 36

7 | **Beinn Odhar** 40

8 | **Stob Binnein** 46

9 | **Ben Venue** 52

10 | **Ben Ledi** 58

Useful Information 64

Scotland's First National Park

In 2002 Loch Lomond and The Trossachs became Scotland's first National Park attracting around 4 million visitors each year. (The Cairngorms became Scotland's second, and so far only other National Park, a year later).

The Park covers an area of 720 square miles and boasts 40 mountains over 2,500 feet in height including some of Scotland's most iconic Munros and Corbetts: Ben Lomond, the craggy peaks of Ben Vorlich and Stuc a Chroin above Loch Earn, big, brutish and beautiful mountains like Ben Lui, Stob Binnein and Cruach Ardrain, and the incomparable Ben Arthur (better known as The Cobbler), to name but a few.

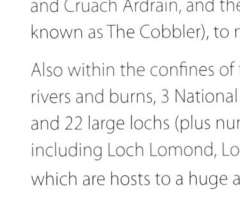

Also within the confines of the National Park are around 50 rivers and burns, 3 National Nature Reserves, 2 Forest Parks and 22 large lochs (plus numerous smaller lochs and lochans), including Loch Lomond, Loch Katrine and Loch Venachar, all of which are hosts to a huge array of wildlife.

Ben Venue panorama

Mountain Walks

The Loch Lomond and The Trossachs National Park straddles the Highland Boundary Fault Line and consequently has a magnificent display of rugged mountains, many rising to over 3,000 feet above sea level.

All within easy reach of Scotland's Central Belt, many of these mountains are regarded as classics, offering exceptional walking, spectacular scenery and plenty of wildlife. Even the mountains that are lower than the ever-popular Munros bestow a day out to rival anywhere else in Britain.

*"Twas there that we parted in yon shady glen,
On the steep, steep side of Ben Lomond,
Where in the purple hue the hieland hills we view,
And the moon coming out in the gloaming."*

'Loch Lomond', Traditional Scottish Folk Song, 1841

TOP 10 WALKS: Mountain Walks

WITH MORE THAN FORTY MOUNTAINS over 2,500 feet spread across the Loch Lomond and The Trossachs National Park, it is tricky to choose just ten favourites. This careful selection aims to illustrate the rich diversity of mountain walks within the National Park.

Classic Munros such as Ben Lomond and Stob Binnein are all visited, while other peaks are combined with near neighbours to provide more challenging walks.

Ben Lomond (Ptarmigan Ridge) page 8

Ben Donich page 14

The Cobbler page 20

Ben Vorlich page 26

An Caisteal — page 30	Cruach Ardrain — page 36
Beinn Odhar — page 40	Stob Binnein — page 46
Ben Venue — page 52	Ben Ledi — page 58

8 ♦ TOP **10** WALKS **LOCH LOMOND & THE TROSSACHS**

Arrochar Alps from Ben Lomond

Walk 1

Ben Lomond (Ptarmigan Ridge)

Rowardennan – Sron Aonaich – Ben Lomond – Bealach Buidhe – Ptarmigan Ridge – Tom Fithich

What to expect:
Excellent path on ascent, rougher path on descent. Steep ascent/descent.

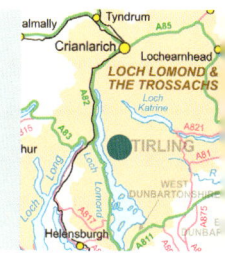

Distance/Time: 12 kilometres/ 7½ miles. Allow 5-6 hours

Ascent/Descent: 943 metres/ 3,094 feet

Start: Ben Lomond Pay & Display car park just north of the Rowardennan Hotel. The car park can get very busy, particularly at weekends

Summits: Ben Lomond   **Grid Ref:** NS 359 986

Ordnance Survey Map: Explorer OL 39 Loch Lomond North *Tyndrum, Crianlarich & Arrochar*

Walk Outline

The outward section of this classic walk can be very busy, with an excellent path climbing all the way from Rowardennan onto Ben Lomond's summit. Steps can be retraced back to Rowardennan, but a far more rewarding (and quieter) return crosses Ptarmigan Ridge. Again, it's along a good path (which can be rough at points) that contains a couple of steep sections, particularly the initial drop from Ben Lomond.

Ben Lomond

Ben Lomond is easily accessed by the huge portion of Scotland's population that resides along its Central Belt. It's one of 46 Munros cared for by the National Trust for Scotland and, in recent years, much work has taken place on the path that helps walkers reach its 974 metre summit every year. Owing to this popularity, Ben Lomond is unfairly judged by many simply as 'Scotland's southernmost Munro', yet it offers some of the finest views within the National Park, and a descent by the scenic Ptarmigan Ridge transforms a great walk into an exceptional one.

Above Loch Lomond

Bog asphodel

TOP 10 WALKS **LOCH LOMOND & THE TROSSACHS**

The Walk

1. From **Rowardennan Car Park**, walk through a gap in a **toilet block** onto the waymarked 'Ben Lomond Access Path' which ascends northeast through rowan, oak and birch woodland. After passing through a gate, the path climbs steadily to a **forestry track**.

Until recently the lower slopes were swathed in conifers, but over the last few years these have been replaced by indigenous species, allowing for more open views and wildlife.

2. Once across the track, continue the ascent above the treeline with the gradient easing for a while.

A stunning vista opens out across Loch Lomond.

After crossing a **footbridge**, the path steepens again, after which it passes through a gate.

Livestock graze on the slopes here so keep dogs on leads.

Beyond another gate, a steep rise climbs north over **Sron Aonaich**, giving the legs a good workout.

Again there are spectacular views along Loch Lomond and, as height is gained, the flatter plains of Stirlingshire appear.

3. A gentler section then proceeds over **open moorland**, home to skylark and meadow pipit, before the path steepens again, zig-zagging uphill towards the main summit ridge, offering fine views of **Ptarmigan Ridge**.

Loch Lomond from Ptarmigan Ridge

4. Now the route travels along perhaps the most dramatic section of the walk, running above **Coire Odhar** and **Coire Fuar**, which drop steeply on either side of the path.

Real care should be taken here in poor visibility during winter, and perhaps into spring, as the edge of the corries may well be heavily corniced. *A marvellous outlook stretches across Loch Ard Forest towards Ben Ledi and Ben Venue.*

Eventually the summit comes into view and a short, gradual climb above the spectacular Coire a' Bhathaich, reaches the 974 metre **summit trig point**.

Only now does the true extent of Ben Lomond's exceptional panorama present itself. The Arrochar Alps (The Cobbler and Beinn Narnain particularly prominent), the big Munros above Crianlarich — Ben More and Stob Binnein — and Arran's celebrated outline are all on show. Loch Lomond sits below, bounded by the rounded Luss Hills.

5. The majority of walkers will retrace steps back to Rowardennan, but for a superb descent it's well worth returning via **Ptarmigan Ridge**.

Panorama taking in Loch Lomond and the Luss Hills

The initial drop to **Bealach Buidhe** is steep and a little exposed at points. Care is required, especially in poor visibility, wet conditions or during winter conditions.

Descend the path that drops steeply northwest from the summit. Soon the exposure lessens but it still drops steeply to Bealach Buidhe at the 750 metre contour, where the incline eases somewhat. From here **flagstones** cross a boggy section, making walking easier.

The path then rises over **Ptarmigan Ridge**, to its high point of 731 metres.

It is a knobbly and undulating ridge, high above Loch Lomond, with a wilder air than that of Ben Lomond's popular 'tourist' path.

Ptarmigan Ridge also gives fabulous views of Ben Lomond's western slopes and south to Loch Lomond and its many islands.

6. The path remains clear as it heads south, dropping steadily and, in a while, leaving the ridge beneath **Tom Fithich**. The straightforward descent continues towards Rowardennan.

7. Once through a gate, the path drops more steeply, eventually running through birch and hawthorn, to another **gate** at the edge of oak woodland.

Once through, follow the path alongside a fast flowing **burn**. When the path forks, keep left and continue to a junction.

8. Go left, cross a **bridge** over the burn onto the **West Highland Way**.

It follows a rough road past **Ben Lomond Cottage** and **Ardress Lodge** to **Rowardennan** to complete the walk. ♦

Camouflaged beauty
Ptarmigan are frequently spotted on the high tops of many of Scotland's mountains. They change their plumage during the year, enabling them to merge perfectly into their surroundings. Their feathers turn white in winter, while during summer a mottled appearance camouflages them against rocks and lichen.

14 ♦ TOP 10 WALKS **LOCH LOMOND & THE TROSSACHS**

Descending from Ben Donich

Walk 2

Ben Donich

Rest and Be Thankful – Gleann Mor – Coire Culach – Ben Donich

Distance/Time: 7.5 kilometres/ 4½ miles. Allow 4 hours
Ascent/Descent: 550 metres/ 1,804 feet
Start: Gleann Mor Forestry Commission car park, 0.5 kilometres southwest of the Rest and Be Thankful
Summits: Ben Donich
Grid Ref: NN 228 069
Ordnance Survey Map: Explorer OL 39 Loch Lomond North Tyndrum, Crianlarich & Arrochar

What to expect:
Good paths along route, with one short scramble. Steep ascent/descent

Walk Outline

At nearly 250 metres above sea level, Gleann Mor, near the Rest and Be Thankful, is an ideal start point for an ascent of Ben Donich. Above the treeline, an excellent path crosses a series of steep climbs to a flatter plateau near Coire Culach. After a short scramble down a crag, the path rises on a steady climb onto the 847 metre summit.

Ben Donich

Surrounded by some of the most popular mountains in the Southern Highlands, Ben Donich is somewhat pushed into the background when compared with neighbouring peaks such as Beinn an Lochain and The Cobbler. And although seemingly retiring in nature, Ben Donich is actually a much more rugged mountain than first impressions suggest when viewed from the Rest and Be Thankful above Glen Croe. Its higher slopes are studded with great crags — one of which requires a little scrambling — with a panorama that is perhaps the finest in the Loch Lomond and The Trossachs National Park.

Views from Ben Donich

Lichen

The Walk

1. The walk begins from the Gleann Mor Forestry Commission car park on the south side of the B828 Lochgoilhead Road, 600 metres southwest of the Rest and Be Thankful car park. *This vantage point provides marvellous views along Glen Croe, which is bounded by craggy mountains such as The Brack and The Cobbler.*

Follow a wide track south through the **car park**, enjoying a fine view of Ben Donich and The Cobbler.

Follow this into **Gleann Mor** (*the Big Glen*) and the **Argyll Forest Park** (ignoring a track on left into Glen Croe) signposted 'Hill Access to Ben Donich'.

After 400 metres the track exits the forest and here turn left onto a waymarked path that then begins to rise steadily above Gleann Mor.

2. The path zigzags uphill, giving good all round views to Beinn Luibhean and Binnein an Fhidhleir. Once through a gate, the path — which can be a little wet and muddy at points — climbs

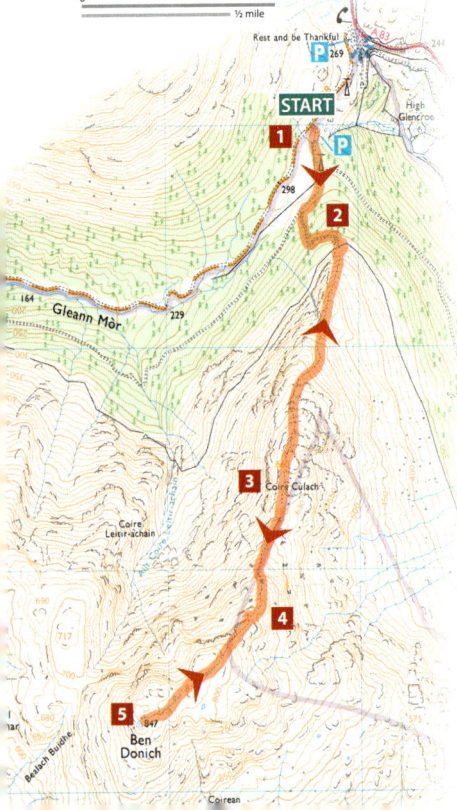

© Crown copyright and/or database right. All rights reserved. Licence number 100047867

Walk 2 – **Ben Donich**

Enjoying amazing views over the Firth of Clyde from Ben Donich

steeply southwest up open hillside onto the northern shoulder of **Ben Donich**.

Here sumptuous views begin to open out to Beinn an Lochain, with little Loch Restil nestled beneath its slopes, and along Gleann Mor to Loch Fyne.

The ridge consists of a series of steep undulations, where height is gained quickly, with the path always clear. It twists and turns uphill with the views changing all the time.

The hillside presents an unfamiliar view of The Cobbler while the conical form of Ben Lomond soon comes in to view. As the route climbs higher Ben Ime appears as does the magnificent outline of Ben Lui.

3. Eventually a flatter section is reached and here the rugged slopes of Ben Donich's upper tier appears with the steep crags of **Coire Culach** dropping from the summit ridge.

There is a fantastic vista along Glen Croe.

Soon another steady climb rises towards the **summit** with the ascent picking its way through craggy outcrops.

A stunning Ben Donich panorama

There are several large, deep crevasses dotted across the slopes where care should be taken. It is best to stick to the path here.

The walk then reaches a **steep crag**, which has a drop of around 15 feet. With a little care and attention the descent down the path and crag causes no real issues but hands and feet will be required — it also has to be climbed on the return journey.

4. The path then continues above steepish slopes before it rises to the left of a large **craggy outcrop**. Beyond this the summit finally comes in to view and it is a simple, gradual climb to reach the 847 metre **trig point**.

The summit plateau is broad, allowing for exploration, with breathtaking views in every direction.

To the south, along the Firth of Clyde, lie the islands of Ailsa Craig, Cumbrae and the stunning profile of Arran. Jura, Islay and Mull complete the set of island views. The awesome sight of Ben Cruachan and Ben Lui dominate the view north and on a clear day the very top of Ben Nevis can be seen.

The Cobbler, Ben Lomond and the Luss Hills look incredible from this vantage point as does Beinn an Lochain. Loch Goil rests way below and Loch Long is also visible.

5. Retrace your outward steps, watching out on the steeper sections, enjoying the wonderful views of the Arrochar Alps, to descend back to the car park to complete the walk. ♦

'Rest and Be Thankful'
The Rest and Be Thankful pass sits at 244 metres above sea level and its name refers to the inscribed stone erected by soldiers when they completed the original military road in the 1750s. Over the centuries the famous viewpoint has provided a welcome break for travellers including Boswell and Johnson, Thomas Pennant and Dorothy and William Wordsworth.

20 ♦ TOP **10** WALKS **LOCH LOMOND & THE TROSSACHS**

The Cobbler

Walk 3

The Cobbler

The Cobbler – Beinn Ime – Beinn Narnain

What to expect:
Clear paths along most of route. Wetter path in glen and on Beinn Ime. Several steep ascents/descents

Distance/Time: 19 kilometres/ 11¾ miles. Allow 7 - 8 hours

Ascent/Descent: 1,497 metres/ 4,911 feet

Start: Succoth pay & display car park on the outskirts of Arrochar. The car park can get very busy, particularly at weekends

Summits: The Cobbler, Beinn Ime, Beinn Narnain

Grid Ref: NN 295 049

Ordnance Survey map: Explorer OL 39 Loch Lomond North *Tyndrum, Crianlarich & Arrochar*

Walk Outline

Excellent paths line the major part of this exemplary route which has several steep ascents. A well constructed path runs through Coire a' Bhalachain to Bealach a' Mhaim from where a tough pull gains The Cobbler. A wet, faint path, rises onto Beinn Ime. After descending back to Bealach a' Mhaim, a generally good path climbs to the summit of Beinn Narnain before the walk returns through Coire a' Bhalachain.

The Cobbler, Beinn Ime & Beinn Narnain

This outstanding traverse summits one Corbett and two Munros. The Cobbler is one of Scotland's most distinctive and distinguished mountains, its triumvirate of peaks unlike anything in the Highlands. Yet, to attain its true summit means threading the exposed eye of the needle, a section not necessarily for the faint hearted. The Munros of Beinn Ime and Beinn Narnain are much easier to reach although the Bealach a' Mhaim, which sits beneath all three mountains, is a little boggy. Whatever summit you stand on, there are a series of incredible vistas, from the Ailsa Craig to Ben Cruachan.

The Cobbler's true summit

Red grouse

The Walk

1. From the **car park at Succoth** — which sits at the northern edge of Loch Long — exit left and carefully cross the busy **A83**. Enter the **Argyll Forest Park** and follow a path up a series of zigzags, through lovely birch woodland.

It rises all the way to a track beside a **bench** where there is a spectacular view over Loch Long to Ben Lomond. Turn left then, after a few metres, just before a **radio mast**, go right onto a path.

This again rises steeply through denser mixed woodland, soon rising above the treeline onto open hillside.

Now you get the first heart-stopping view of The Cobbler, its unique profile dominating the aspect ahead.

2. A superb path now continues on a gradual ascent, allowing you to catch your breath and enjoy the fabulous surroundings.

Keep on northwest above the fast flowing **Allt a' Bhalachain**. Beside a **weir** the path splits so keep right and continue on, in due course reaching the enormous **Narnain Boulders**.

3. Soon afterwards the path forks and again keep right, cutting a course through **Coire**

© Crown copyright and/or database right. All rights reserved. Licence number 100047867

Walk 3 – **The Cobbler** ♦ 23

Looking down over Ben Lomond from Beinn Ime

a' Bhalachain, inbetween the slopes of The Cobbler and Beinn Narnain.

The main path ends at the head of **Bealach a' Mhaim** beside a **marker post** (GR NN 261 065).

It is a marvellous spot with a real sense of wildness and views extending to Beinn Ime, Beinn Luibhean and Beinn an Lochain.

4. Make a left from where an excellent, but steep, path rises south up the northern shoulder of The Cobbler.

Fabulous views open out to the west and eventually the gradient relents to reach a **col** inbetween the North and Central Peaks.

Go left and climb onto the **North Peak** with the final metres crossing awkward **rocky slabs**, which are tricky, especially on the descent.

When on top, the view is exceptional, with the Central Peak drawing the eye towards the Firth of Clyde, Arran and Ailsa Craig.

Return to the **col** then make the final steady ascent onto the **Central Peak** with only the intrepid 'threading the eye' to gain the true summit.

A stunning panorama spreads out far below the summit of The Cobbler

5. Return to **Bealach a' Mhaim** then head north along a rough path, across **boggy ground** towards Beinn Ime.

The path becomes faint but soon reaches a gate. Once through, the path rises over open hillside, on a tough ascent, eventually running right of a burn, to reach a junction beside a small **marker cairn**.

Turn left over the **burn**. The path improves as it climbs steadily northwest to gain **Beinn Ime's** rugged 1,011 metre top, the highest point of the walk.

Another wonderful outlook extends over Ben Lomond, Loch Arklet and Loch Katrine.

6. Return to the gate near the base of Beinn Ime. Once through keep straight on, heading southeast-east along a faint path, which becomes clearer as ground rises towards Beinn Narnain.

Around the 700 metre contour, pass a path on the right (marked with a very **small cairn**), which is for the descent.

Now a well-worn path rises steeply east, bestowing fabulous views back towards Beinn Ime.

Soon the path runs along Beinn Narnain's southern slopes before veering northeast, through **bouldery ground**, to reach **Beinn Narnain's summit**

Walk 3 – **The Cobbler**

plateau. A trig sits just east of the large **summit cairn**.

7. Return to the path marked with the **small cairn** and turn left.

8. A path contours the lower slopes of Beinn Narnain, dropping southwest back to the outward-bound path at the base of The Cobbler. Turn left and retrace your steps back to **Succoth** to complete the walk. ♦

Big, big boulders

The enormous Narnain Boulders are two glacial erratics which provide clues to the geological events that helped form this topographical masterpiece. They also played a central role in the great outdoor movement of the 1930s. Men and women looking to escape Glasgow's industrial backdrop would head north after finishing work on a Saturday, to spend Sunday climbing the Arrochar Alps and camping beneath the Narnain Boulders.

Ben Vorlich

Walk 4

Ben Vorlich

Inveruglas – Loch Sloy Dam Road – Coiregrogain – Ben Vorlich

What to expect:
Very steep climb onto Ben Vorlich's ridge. Rough path to/from ridge and clear ridge path to summit.

Distance/Time: 13.25 kilometres/ 8¼ miles. Allow 5 - 6 hours
Ascent/Descent: 928 metres/ 3,045 feet
Start: Inveruglas Visitor Centre pay & display car park
Summits: Ben Vorlich
Grid Ref: NN 322 098
Ordnance Survey Map: Explorer OL 39 Loch Lomond North *Tyndrum, Crianlarich & Arrochar*

Walk Outline

An ascent of Ben Vorlich above Loch Lomond is tough with one particularly steep section. A tarmaced section of the Cowal Way offers a straightforward approach towards Loch Sloy before a path, which is faint and rough at points, gains Ben Vorlich's southern ridge. From here a clear path rises gradually to the summit. The simplest return is by the route of ascent.

Ben Vorlich

Ben Vorlich is the northernmost Arrochar Alp and shouldn't be confused with the National Park's other Ben Vorlich (also a Munro) that rises above Loch Earn. Our Ben Vorlich climbs to 943 metres above Loch Lomond and dominates the landscape to the north of Tarbet.

It is a rugged and robust mountain — its translation from Gaelic may mean *Mountain of the Big Loch* or *Big Stony Mountain*, both of which make sense — and to reach its summit entails one very steep, yet straightforward climb.

Its position within the Southern Highlands means Ben Vorlich offers fabulous views.

Vorlich view

Ring ouzel

The Walk

1. An ascent of Ben Vorlich begins from the **shores of Loch Lomond** at **Inveruglas Visitor Centre**.

Carefully cross the **A82**, turn left and follow a section of the **Cowal Way**, passing the **huge pipes** of the **Loch Sloy Power Station**.

2. After 800 metres the path culminates at narrow road. Bear right, go through a gate and follow the road underneath a **railway bridge** after which it sweeps right then left, climbing steadily through open countryside. The conical shape of Ben Vane comes into view.

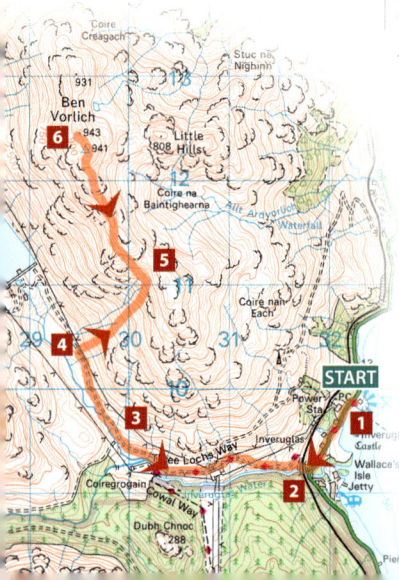

Beyond an **electricity substation** *further fine views extend to A' Chrois, one of the smaller Arrochar Alp peaks.*

The road then levels off and continues above **Inveruglas Water**, soon passing, on the left, the access road to Coiregrogain (where The Cowal Way continues its journey).

3. After passing a track on the left, the road ascends gradually towards the impressive engineering feat of **Loch Sloy Dam**. Keep on for approximately 900 metres.

4. At this point look out for a **small cairn** on the right of the road, just after a **burn**, which marks the point to begin the climb onto Ben Vorlich.

Take the faint path that begins a relentlessly steep climb of approximately 600 metres in just over 2 kilometres.

As height is gained the path becomes clearer. *There are fabulous views down into the glen below and towards Ben Vane, and Loch Sloy.*

The route is straightforward (just keep climbing northeast) yet it's tough. Mercifully, the **south ridge of Ben Vorlich** is eventually gained where the incline eases.

Looking north from the top of Ben Vorlich

5. From here a gradual uphill pull northwest along the ridge soon reaches a **trig point**.

However, a final climb is still required as the 943 metres **true summit** is still a short distance ahead.

Upon reaching the top many of the Arrochar Alps vie for attention while the outlook across Loch Lomond to Ben Lomond and the Luss Hills is superb. Ben Lui and Ben Cruachan are also visible.

6. The simplest return is via the route of ascent, taking care on the steep descent, after which it is an easy walk along the road back to Inveruglas, to complete the walk. ♦

Water power

The construction of Loch Sloy Hydroelectric Power Station began in 1945 and it was opened five years later. Such was the scale of the project that camps were built near Ben Vorlich to house the workforce, which included German prisoners of war. Loch Sloy Dam is 56 metres high and 357 metres long. Twenty-one men lost their lives during the construction of the dam.

The Southern Highlands from Twistin Hill

Walk 5

An Caisteal

Glen Falloch – Sron Garbh – Twistin Hill – An Caisteal – Bealach Buidhe – Beinn a' Chroin – Stob Ghlas Beag

Distance/Time: 14.5 kilometres/ 9 miles. Allow 6 - 7 hours

Ascent/Descent: 987 metres/ 3,238 feet

Start: Large lay-by, S side of A82, 2.5 kilometres SW of Crianlarich

Summits: An Caisteal, Beinn a' Chroin

Grid ref: NN 369 239

Ordnance Survey Map: Explorer OL 39 Loch Lomond North Tyndrum, Crianlarich & Arrochar

What to expect:
Clear paths on tops, short scramble onto Beinn a' Chroin. Some muddy paths, especially on return route

Walk Outline
A steep, muddy path climbs onto Sron Garbh. Once on the ridge, a superb path rises over Sron Garbh and Twistin Hill onto An Caisteal. The path drops steeply to Bealach Buidhe before ascending onto Beinn a' Chroin — however hands and feet are required on a short scramble just beneath the summit. After another steep descent down Stob Ghlas Beag, a wet path slows the return through a glen.

An Caisteal & Beinn a' Chroin
An Caisteal and Beinn a' Chroin combine for a tough but hugely absorbing walk over two of the National Park's most rugged Munros. There is lots of ascent and descent, some of it steep. The wonderful ridge walk from Sron Garbh up Twistin Hill onto An Caisteal is perhaps the finest section of the route where the views are magnificent. Beinn a' Chroin's large summit plateau is worth exploration with further extensive vistas stretching in all directions, including that of Ben More and Stob Binnein. On a clear day Ben Nevis and the mountains of the Isle of Mull are visible.

Ascending Sron Garbh

Wheatear

The Walk

1. *The lay-by start point has room for a number of cars but it can get very busy as it serves a number of walks in the area.*

Climb a stile onto a gravel path and follow this underneath a **railway bridge** onto a track that crosses a **bridge** over the **River Falloch**.

The steep slopes of Sron Garbh rise above with its lower reaches scattered with Scots pine.

The track climbs gradually for just over 1.25 kilometres, passing through two gates.

2. Immediately after the second gate turn right onto a narrow path and begin to climb steadily southwest.

Here there is a marvellous view across Glen Falloch to Ben Challum.

As height is gained the path is a little vague at points (a close eye would have to kept on it in poor visibility) and boggy but the ascent is reasonably straightforward. A couple of sections of slabby rock may require hands.

The prolonged ascent eventually gains **Sron Garbh's rugged little ridge**.

A wonderful view opens out across much of the Southern Highlands, including the neighbouring Munros of Beinn Chabhair, Cruach Ardrain, Ben More and Stob Binnein.

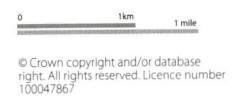

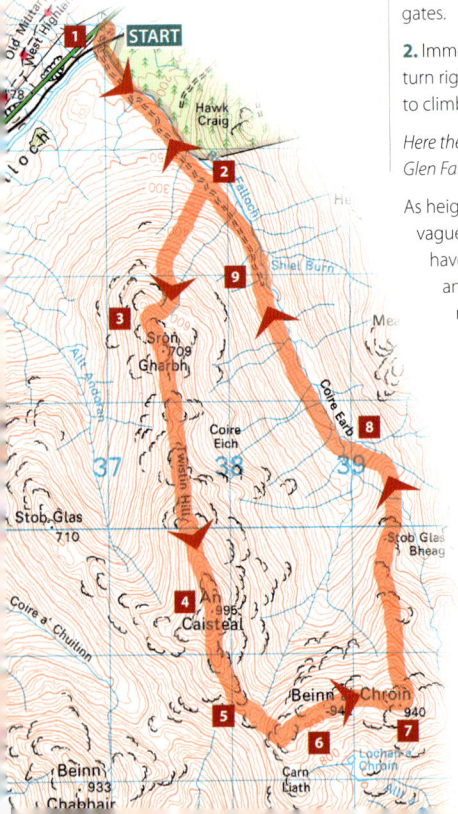

© Crown copyright and/or database right. All rights reserved. Licence number 100047867

Walk 5 – **An Caisteal** ♦ 33

Glen Falloch from Beinn a Chroin

3. A clear, firm path now rises south onto the 709 metre top of Sron Garbh, granting a fine view of An Caisteal's distinctive profile — its name simply means *The Castle*. A fabulous section of the walk now begins.

Beyond Sron Garbh the walk climbs steadily again, heading south onto the **ridge of Twistin Hill.** This route is clear and travels across exceptional scenery.

Approaching the summit there is one, short but awkward spot with a short dip before a climb, or easy scramble, where again hands are required.

After this it is a final, short climb onto the 995 metre **summit of An Caisteal**, the highest point of the walk.

This offers an outstanding vantage point to look onto The Cobbler and along Loch Long. Ben Vorlich, Stuc a Chroin, Ben Venue, Ben Lomond and Ben Cruachan are all visible, as is Ben More above Crianlarich and, on a clear day, its namesake on Mull. There is also a good view of Beinn a' Chroin's long summit ridge.

4. The path now drops steeply south then south south-east from An Caisteal.

Cruach Ardrain, Beinn Tulaichean and Stob Binnein from Beinn a' Chroin's summit

It can be a little eroded at points and care should be taken on the steeper sections.

It drops down to **Bealach Buidhe** at the base of Beinn a' Chroin.

5. From here, a steep climb leads up the **western edge of Beinn a' Chroin**, the path running close to steep-ish drops on the right.

It soon sweeps left after which there is a short but awkward **scramble** up a steep slope.

Beyond this, a final steady rise northeast gains **Beinn a' Chroin's summit ridge**.

6. Continue northeast across the expansive ridge, in full view of Ben More, Stob Binnein, Cruach Ardrain and Beinn Tulaichean.

After passing two cairns the path drops east then rises again to gain **Beinn a' Chroin's 940 metre top** at the eastern edge of the ridge.

A marvellous panorama takes in the Ben Lawers massif, the Arrochar Alps, and the peaks of Glencoe and Ben Nevis.

7. A faint path drops north from the summit and begins a long descent, winding down the scenic, defined **ridge of Stob Ghlas Beag** — it is eroded on

Walk 5 – **An Caisteal** ♦ 35

steeper sections — eventually dropping down to the base of a glen.

8. Once across **two burns**, a faint path (which is sometimes nonexistent) heads along the west bank of the **River Falloch**'s early stages. The ground slows progress until, after 2 kilometres, a firm track is reached.

9. This provides an easy descent onto the outward-bound route, which is followed back to the start, to complete the walk. ♦

Scots pine

Several stands of Scots pine can be spotted on the lower slopes of Sron Garbh. These iconic trees can live for around 300 years and are immediately recognisable by their gnarled, twisted trunks, orangey bark and broad spread of upper foliage. After the last Ice Age Scots pine were prevalent across much of Britain but today their natural range is confined to the Highlands of Scotland.

36 ♦ TOP **10** WALKS **LOCH LOMOND & THE TROSSACHS**

Approaching Cruach Ardrain's northwest ridge

Walk 6

Cruach Ardrain

Glen Falloch – Grey Height – Meall Dhamh – Cruach Ardrain – Beinn Tulaichean – Coire Earb – Meall Dhamh – Grey Height

What to expect:
Good paths along most of route. Section of pathless ground. Steep ascent/descent

Distance/Time: 15.25 kilometres/ 9½ miles miles. Allow 6 - 7 hours
Ascent/Descent: 1,035 metres/ 3,396 feet
Start: Large lay-by, S side of A82, 2.5 kilometres SW of Crianlarich
Summits: Cruach Ardrain, Beinn Tulaichean
Grid Ref: NN 369 2397
Ordnance Survey Map: Explorer OL 39 Loch Lomond North *Tyndrum, Crianlarich & Arrochar*

Walk Outline
Good paths line the majority of a straightforward route onto Cruach Ardrain and Beinn Tulaichean. From Glen Falloch, grassy slopes soon gain a path that leads over Grey Height and Meall Dhamh after which it continues onto Cruach Ardrain. A steep descent then a steady climb easily gains Beinn Tulaichean. A traverse of the slopes above Coire Earb returns to Meall Dhamh and then Glen Falloch.

Cruach Ardrain & Beinn Tulaichean
The mountains of Cruach Ardrain and Beinn Tulaichean form part of a chain of mountains, above Crianlarich, that include Stob Binnein, Beinn a Chroin and An Caisteal. To reach Beinn Tulaichean's summit from Cruach Ardrain requires only another 350 feet or so of ascent and as a result it's seen, somewhat disparagingly by many, as just another 'tick' off the Munro list. However it offers fine views of the surrounding peaks. Cruach Ardrain's simple derivation is the *High Stacked Heap*, while Beinn Tulaichean's lumpy outline (when viewed from Inverlochlarig) translates from Gaelic as *Hill of the Hillock*.

View from Cruach Ardrain

Mountain hare

The Walk

1. The **lay-by** start point has room for several cars but it can get very busy as it serves a number of walks in the area.

Once over a stile, a gravel path goes under a **railway bridge** onto a track that crosses a bridge over the **River Falloch**.

A gradual climb of 1.25 kilometres passes the edge of a **conifer plantation**. Here bear left and drop down to cross the **River Falloch** via a **footbridge**.

2. Keeping to the right of the plantation and a deer fence, ascend grassy slopes for just under 1 kilometre to a clear path.

3. Bear right and follow the path southeast as it rises easily over **Grey Height**, where marvellous views open out north to Ben Challum. The path then extends up a broad ridge to gain the rocky **top of Meall Dhamh**.

At 814 metres in height it offers a superb outlook, one that takes in An Caisteal and Beinn a Chroin.

4. Although the path remains clear, it now picks its way over a series of rocky lumps to a **shallow col**, where the ground ascends to reach the base of Cruach Ardrain's northwest ridge.

From here the path climbs over steep, grassy slopes, in an easterly direction, onto **Cruach Ardrain's southwest top**, which is marked with **two cairns**. A shallow dip and a short climb finally gains its 1046 metre **apex**.

A wonderful view awaits with the rocky profiles of Ben More, Stob Binnein, Beinn a Chroin and An Caisteal surrounding Cruach Ardrain. Beinn Tulaichean's shapely outline sits just below.

5. For Beinn Tulaichean, retrace steps past the two cairns from where a path descends sharply down **Cruach Ardrain's southeast ridge** to a **bealach**.

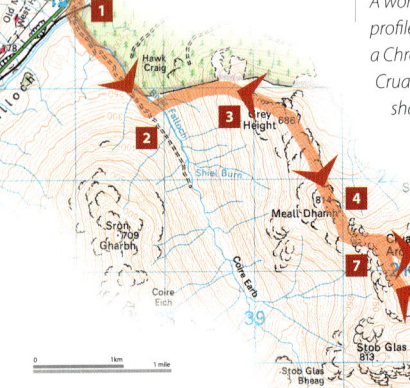

Looking towards Cruach Ardrain from Meall Dhamh

From here a simple, steady rise quickly leads onto the top of **Beinn Tulaichean**.

At 946 metres, it is 100 metres lower than Cruach Ardrain but still offers marvellous views down into Inverlochlarig and east to the prominent twin peaks of Ben Vorlich and Stuc a Chroin.

6. Return to the bealach in between the two mountains. However, rather than ascending back to Cruach Ardrain, leave the path and head northwest, traversing the **southern slope of Cruach Ardrain**, above **Coire Earb**. This returns you to the path beneath **Meall Dhamh's southeastern face**.

7. From here, retrace your steps over **Meall Dhamh** and **Grey Height** back to the start, to complete the walk. ♦

Hidden glen?

Glen Falloch is a delightful glen — cut in two by the River Falloch — that runs southwest from Crianlarich to Loch Lomond. The glen's upper reaches, near the slopes of Cruach Ardrain, are studded with gorgeous stands of Scots Pine, while further down the glen is the Falls of Falloch, a spectacular waterfall some 30 feet in height. Glen Falloch is thought to mean the Glen of Hiding.

40 ♦ TOP 10 WALKS **LOCH LOMOND & THE TROSSACHS**

Meall Bhuide and the distant Crianlarich Munros from Beinn Odhar

Walk 7

Beinn Odhar

Tyndrum – West Highland Way – Beinn Odhar – Lochan Choire Dhuibh – Meall Buidhe

Distance/Time: 8.5 kilometres/ 5¼ miles. Allow 4½ hours

Ascent/Descent: 708 metres/ 2,323 feet

Start: Large car park at The Green Welly Stop or Tyndrum iCentre car park

Summits: Beinn Odhar, Meall Buidhe

Grid Ref: NN 329 304

Ordnance Survey Map: Explorer OL 39 Loch Lomond North *Tyndrum, Crianlarich & Arrochar*

What to expect:
Much of the route is pathless. Steep ascent onto Beinn Odhar and from Meall Buidhe

Walk Outline

Due to the predominantly pathless nature of this route, an ascent of Beinn Odhar and Meall Buidhe is one of the toughest in the guidebook. A section of the West Highland Way leads to the base of Beinn Odhar from where steep grassy slopes climb to the summit. A line of wooden posts runs across a high plateau onto Meall Buidhe. A steep descent returns to the West Highland Way.

Beinn Odhar and Meall Buidhe

At 2,956 feet in height Beinn Odhar is only 44 feet short of Munro status; it is therefore classed as a Corbett. Consequently, its slopes are quiet and an ascent has a wilder air to it. Beinn Odhar (*Dun Coloured Hill*) is usually tackled as part of the Tyndrum Five Corbetts but this is a massive undertaking. Therefore, a far more enjoyable route climbs Beinn Odhar before crossing a marvellous windswept plateau onto Meall Buidhe (*Yellow Hill*). Surrounded by higher, better-known peaks these two under-rated mountains provide stunning views towards the likes of Ben Lui and Stob Binnein.

Snow on Ben Odhar

Golden eagle

The Walk

1. From either **car park** in the centre of **Tyndrum**, follow the pavement northwest alongside the **A82**, crossing a **bridge over Crom Allt**. After this turn right onto the **West Highland Way**, beside a mini-market and continue onto a narrow road.

At its end keep straight on along a track, climbing gradually past **Tyndrum Cemetery**. Once through a gate, the **West Highland Way** continues north, with Beinn Odhar's rounded dome rising ahead.

The **Crom Allt** rushes downhill below, its banks flanked with birch and rowan.

2. After 1.25 kilometres the track crosses a lovely **old stone bridge** over a **burn** before crossing a **railway bridge**. Beyond a gate continue for another 100 metres then leave the West Highland Way by bearing right onto the **lower grassy slopes of Beinn Odhar**, beside two old metal fenceposts.

3. From here a steady climb northeast begins over a series of knobbly grassy knolls, with only the faint outline of a path, which soon peters out. The ground can be a little wet at first but the gradient is less imposing than it looks from Tyndrum.

Fine views open out to the Munros of Beinn Dubhcraig and Ben Oss, and the Corbett of Beinn Breac-laith. Ben Lui's magnificent profile comes into view as height is gained.

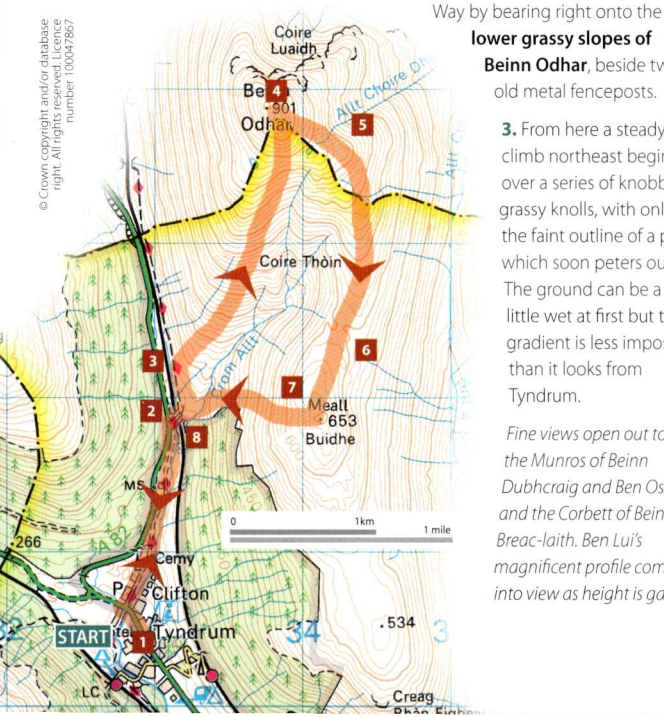

The Crom Allt and West Highland Way approaching Beinn Odhar

Higher up, a wonderful view across Meall Buidhe to Stob Binnein and Ben More appears. Flora such as tormentil and harebell may also be spotted.

The ground underfoot eventually becomes a little drier as the grassy slopes become scattered with rocks. A vein of **slabby rock** and then a **stony track** leads higher still.

<u>**Old mine shafts** are dotted across the hillside and should not be entered.</u>

The gradient eases for a short time as the route passes a **lochan**, leading to a final steep climb. There are a couple of **boulderfields** to cross where care should be taken, but **Beinn Odhar's 901 metre summit** marked with a small **cairn** is soon gained.

The outlook is magnificent. Coire Luaidh drops steeply into Glen Coralan then onto Beinn Dorain with the slopes of Beinn a' Caisteal drawing the eye to Loch Lyon. The peaks of Glen Etive and Glencoe are visible on a clear day, while the Crianlarich mountains form a formidable view to the south.

Beinn a Chaisteil and Loch Lyon from Beinn Odhar

4. From the summit it is an initially steep descent, over pathless ground where good navigation is required in poor visibility. Take a southeast bearing and follow this down to little **Lochan Choire Dhuibh**.

5. Now the gradient eases a little as the route continues southeast across pathless ground, eventually reaching the **main ridge connecting Beinn Odhar with Meall Buidhe**.

Once on the ridge a **line of posts** provide a good handrail. Keep on above **Coire Thoin** with the broad ridge veering south to cross its lowest point (603 metres).

6. Underfoot it is very boggy but the posts provide a route to avoid the worst sections. It is then a gradual, straightforward climb onto **Meall Buidhe** (the posts end before the summit).

There is now another sumptuous view — Beinn Odhar's profile from this angle is particularly attractive.

7. From Meall Buidhe head west with the incline steepening as a **conifer plantation** comes into view. The initial descent is steep, dropping down grassy slopes requiring care.

Carefully descend to the northern

corner of the forest, cross a narrow **burn** and then follow the **forest edge** west, descending steadily down to **Crom Allt**.

8. At its widest point a crossing is fairly straightforward, after which return to the **West Highland Way** beside the railway bridge. Retrace your steps back to **Tyndrum** to complete the walk. ♦

Lead mines

Lead was mined in the glens and on the mountains surrounding Tyndrum from the early 18th century and the open remains of several mine shafts are dotted around Beinn Odhar's upper slopes. Sir Robert Clifton began mining in Tyndrum in 1730 after which a succession of operators continued production, including The Scots Mining Company and The Earls of Breadalbane. Lead mining finally ceased here in 1926.

46 ♦ TOP 10 WALKS **LOCH LOMOND & THE TROSSACHS**

Stob Binnein from Stob Coire an Lochain

Walk 8

Stob Binnein

Inverlochlarig – Stob Invercarnaig – Creag Artair – Na Staidhrichean – Stob Coire an Lochain – Stob Binnein

What to expect:
Clear path for most of route. Section of pathless ground. Very steep ascent/descent

Distance/Time: 9.75 kilometres/ 6 miles. Allow 5 hours
Ascent/Descent: 1,055 metres/ 3,461 feet
Start: Car park near Inverlochlarig, 9.75 km west of Balquhidder
Summits: Stob Binnein
Grid Ref: NN 446 185
Ordnance Survey Map: Explorer Explorer OL46 Callander, Aberfoyle & Lochearnhead, Balquhidder & Strathyre

Walk Outline

This magnificent out-and-back walk has some steep climbs, including the relentless rise from Inverlochlarig to Stob Invercarnaig. Beyond this, however, a magnificent walk heads over Creag Artair and Stob Coire an Lochain onto Stob Binnein's 1165m summit. Apart from one marshy section between Stob Invercarnaig and Creag Artair, the path is clear throughout. The ridge from Na Staidhrichean onto Stob Binnein may well be corniced well into spring.

Stob Binnein

Stob Binnein is one of Scotland's finest and most popular mountains. Its shapely outline can be seen from a number of points across the Southern Highlands along with its near neighbour, the slightly higher Ben More. Climbing from Inverlochlarig means expending some energy initially but it is worth the effort as Stob Binnein offers an outstanding mountain walk with incredible views in all directions. The name Stob Binnein may translate from Gaelic as *The Anvil*, which would correlate with its conspicuous flat top, but its definition seems to be far more prosaic, simply meaning *The Peak*.

Stob Binnein from Ben More

Dotterel

The Walk

1. *Inverlochlarig car park is at the end of a 9.75 kilometre single track road that runs from Balquhidder alongside beautiful Loch Voil and Loch Doine. The car park can be busy, particularly at weekends, as it serves a number of local hill walks.*

From the **car park**, cross the road then a stile, signed for 'Am Binnein (*the historic name for Stob Binnein*), Stob Coire an Lochan and Ben More'. A very steep, **sustained climb** now begins, along a well worn, at times muddy, path.

The path helps on this stage of the ascent and, as height is gained quickly, superb views open out to Stob Breac, Stob a Choin and down onto Inverlochlarig Farm.

As the path winds its way up north towards Stob Invercarnaig further fine views, particularly that of the River Larig, snaking its way through Balquhidder Glen, open out.

After a while the path approaches a fence, where the gradient eases a little. Once over a stile it then steepens again as the path heads northeast beneath and around the **crags of Stob Invercarnaig**.

© Crown copyright and/or database right. All rights reserved. Licence number 100047867

Walk 8 – **Stob Binnein** ♦ 49

A cloud-capped Stob a Choin from above Inverlochlarig

Once across a **burn** the path veers north above **Stob Invercarnaig**.

Here there is a spectacular view along Loch Doine and Loch Voil to the twin peaks of Ben Vorlich and Stuc a Chroin.

2. At this point the path peters out as it climbs gradually across open hillside, with much of the ground marshy – good navigation would be required in poor visibility. Keep in a northerly direction, the gradient steepening a little as it makes its way up and onto the rounded **crest of Creag Artair**.

3. In clear weather the route can be seen ahead with a good path crossing the wonderful **high plateau of Na Staidhrichean**, with the flowing line of the ridge drawing the eye towards Stob Coire an Lochain.

In winter, and often well into spring, this section of the route may be heavily corniced, and in poor visibility it would be advisable to stay away from the steep slopes on either side of the ridge.

It is also a wonderfully scenic section of the walk, on a pleasant incline after the energy sapping ascent.

Stob Binnein's incredible profile from Stob Coire an Lochain

Sumptuous views extend across Inverlochlarig Glen to the Munros of Beinn Tulaichean and Cruach Ardrain. Ben Ledi is prominent to the south.

The path heads north-northwest, leading to a steadier pull from where the ridge narrows a little, giving a real feeling of height — *the views now extend to Loch Tay and the Ben Lawers massif and across much of Perthshire and Stirlingshire*. Keep on to reach **Stob Coire an Lochain**.

The view to Stob Binnein's beautiful outline is stunning from this position. Dotterel, skylark and, perhaps, mountain hare may well be spotted on this wild plateau.

4. Once past the **lochan** that gives Stob Coire an Lochain its name, a **short dip** leads to the final climb. The well-worn path now steepens considerably and zigzags upwards, the final section through **rocky slabs**, to reach **Stob Binnien's magnificent 1,165 metre summit**.

The top is marked with a **small cairn** from where extend a number of massive views — *the craggy peaks of Beinn a Chroin, An Caisteal and Cruach Ardrain sit to the west, the four big Munros of the Ben Lui group rise to the northwest, while the huge bulk of Ben More seems almost close enough to touch. Simply put it is one of the*

Walk 8 – **Stob Binnein** ♦ 51

finest views in the Loch Lomond and The Trossachs National Park.

5. The only feasible return is by the means of ascent. The descent is marvellous, with fantastic views of the Southern Highlands throughout. Upon returning to **Stob Invercarnaig** however, care should be taken on the knee crunching descent back to the start, to complete the walk. ♦

Rob Roy

Rob Roy MacGregor, one of Scotland's most famous historical figures, lived part of his life at Inverlochlarig, and may have died here in 1734. He was born in 1671 at Glengyle, beside Loch Katrine, and was involved in the Jacobite uprising of 1688. He became a folk hero, chiefly because of his feud with the 1st Duke of Montrose. Rob Roy is buried in Balquhidder Kirkyard.

Winter conditions on Ben Venue

Walk 9

Ben Venue

Loch Achray – Pass of Achray – Gleann Riabhach – Bealach Mor na Beinne – Bealach na h-Imriche – Ben Venue

What to expect:
Excellent path along most of route. Wetter ground beneath summit. Some steep ascents/descents

Distance/Time: 14.5 kilometres/ 9 miles. Allow 5 - 6 hours

Ascent/Descent: 695 metres/ 2,280 feet

Start: Ben Venue Pay & Display Car Park, which sits on the west side of the A821, 9.5km north of Aberfoyle

Summits: Ben Venue   **Grid Ref:** NN 505 068

Ordnance Survey Map: Explorer OL 46 The Trossachs, *Callander, Aberfoyle & Lochearnhead, Balquhidder & Strathyre*

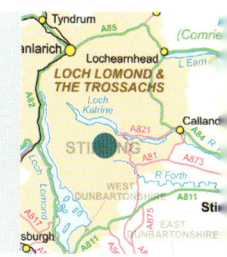

Walk Outline

It is a long steady pull onto the twin-topped Ben Venue. An excellent path rises from Loch Achray and through the secluded Gleann Riabhach onto a flatter plateau above Bealach Mor na Beinne and Bealach na h-Imriche. Another climb gains a col between the two summits after which the path climbs onto both. The return is by the route of ascent.

Ben Venue

Ben Venue is an incredibly rugged mountain, one that rises to 729 metres above Loch Katrine, deep in the heart of The Trossachs. Ben Venue commands a central position within the National Park and the surrounding mountains, including Ben Ledi and Ben Lomond, are bigger. This gives rise to Ben Venue's derivation of *the Small Mountain*. However a climb onto its summit shouldn't be underestimated, but the exertion required to reach the top is worth the effort as the panorama is truly exceptional, taking in a number of muscular peaks, gorgeous lochs and even the Wallace Monument above Stirling.

Ben Venue summit

Buzzard

Exceptional views extend across Loch Katrine to the Arrochar Alps from Ben Venue

The Walk

1. There are a number of twists and turns along the lower reaches of this route but it is well waymarked. The start point offers marvellous views along Loch Achray.

Take the path at the back of the **car park** and follow this through attractive woodland — *where, immediately, there is a superb view of Ben Venue's rugged ridge.*

After a gentle descent, turn left at a junction (signed 'Ben Venue Hill Path') and continue through the glorious landscape of The Trossachs. Once across a section of **boardwalk** the path culminates at the Loch Katrine Trossachs Pier road.

2. Turn left onto a side road for Loch Katrine Dam and follow this through the **Pass of Achray** and alongside the **Achray Water**, *where dippers may be spotted.*

After 600 metres, turn left onto a waymarked path, which drops down to cross a **bridge** over the river beside an impressive **waterfall**. It then rises steeply to a forest track. Keep right, continue for another 330 metres and here leave the track for a waymarked path on the left.

3. After another couple of steep climbs go right onto a path, which rises to another forest track. Turn left then, after 170 metres, go right from where a path rises steadily *and offers fine views of Beinn an Fhogharaidh's long rocky ridge and of Ben A'an's pointed peak.*

Upon gaining a track go left then immediately right from where the path now continues west above the lovely, secluded **Gleann Riabhach** (*the Brindled Glen*), *offering a distant view of Ben Ledi.*

4. It is now a nice gradual pull up through the glen *with superb views of Loch Achray and the eastern flanks of Stob an Lochain. Raven and buzzard may be spotted floating on the thermals above.*

In a while the path curves right and rises a little more steeply north — with Ben Venue's southern slopes and its rugged ridge coming into view — all the way to the **base of a steep headwall at the top of the glen**. *An impressive waterfall plummets from the slopes.*

Continue by zigzagging uphill on a **well-engineered path**.

Until recently this section was very boggy but walking is now relatively simple, with only a short section of **rocky slabs** a little awkward.

© Crown copyright and/or database right. All rights reserved.
Licence number 100047867

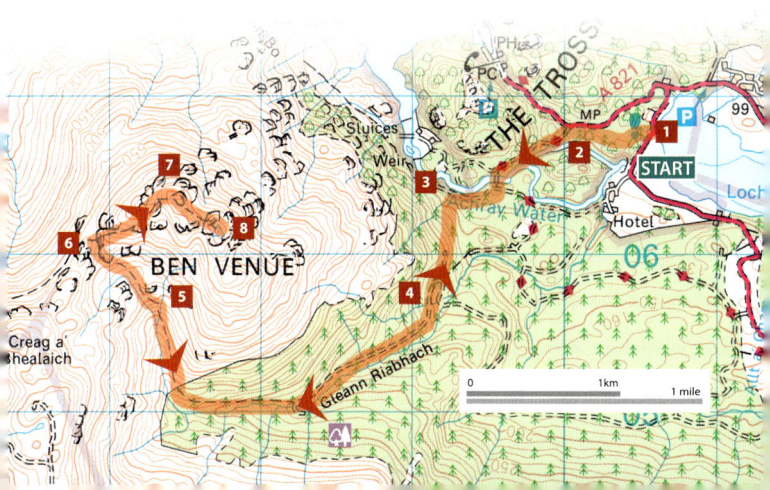

Loch Katrine panorama from the summit of Ben Venue

5. Climb to a flatter section of **plateau beneath the main ridge of Ben Venue**, inbetween **Bealach Mor na Beinne** and **Bealach na h-Imriche**. The path picks its way northwest across a wetter section to reach a **cairn** at the 580 metre contour.

6. Just after the cairn bear right where a path rises steeply northeast up through a **rocky landscape**. Soon the incline eases and continues gradually towards the **summit ridge**. *The outlook begins to open out, giving an idea of the panorama that awaits at the top.*

After a short descent to a boggy section ascend east, beneath the southern edge of the summit.

Just beneath the top bear left from where a short pull gains the compact 729 metre **top of Ben Venue** and a truly exceptional view.

Ben Lomond, the Arrochar Alps, Ben Lui, the Crianlarich Munros all frame Loch Katrine and Loch Arklet below. On a clear day Tinto Hill, the Culter Fells and Arran are all also visible.

7. To take in the **second, slightly lower 727 metre top**, descend then reascend southwest to reach the **trig point**.

Another outstanding panorama extends across Loch Venachar and Ben Ledi to the Ochil Hills, the Campsie Fells, Stirling Castle and the Wallace Monument.

8. The only feasible means of retreat is to retrace your steps back through Gleann Riabhach to the Pass of Achray and a simple return to the start, to complete the walk. ♦

Mountain ravens

They may not have the power and romanticism of the golden eagle but the raven is still a splendid bird. Jet-black in appearance, bigger than a buzzard and with a thick neck and powerful bill, the raven is perfectly adapted to defend its territory. Breeding normally takes place on cliffs or overhanging crags while food and water for their young is carried in a throat pouch.

58 ♦ TOP 10 WALKS **LOCH LOMOND & THE TROSSACHS**

The lower slopes of Beinn an t-Sidhein give a fantastic view along Loch Lubnaig

Walk 10

Ben Ledi

Pass of Leny – Meall Odhar – Ben Ledi – Bealach nan Corp – Stank Glen

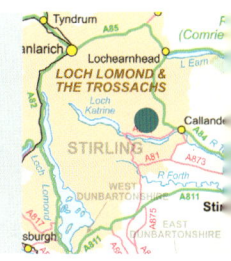

Distance/Time: 10 kilometres/ 6¼ miles. Allow 5 hours
Ascent/Descent: 744 metres/ 2,441 feet
Start: Car park at the end of a minor road off the A84, on the western bank of Garbh Uisge, 3km west of Kilmahog
Summits: Ben Ledi
Grid Ref: NN 587 091
Ordnance Survey Map: Explorer OL 46 The Trossachs, *Callander, Aberfoyle & Lochearnhead, Balquhidder & Strathyre*

What to expect:
Clear path on ascent, fainter path on descent into Stank Glen. Clear path through glen

Walk Outline
The ascent of Ben Ledi is along a well-constructed path, with some steepish pulls, particularly up the mountain's lower reaches. A gradual then steep rise leads over Meall Odhar to Ben Ledi's summit. The path can be a little vague at points on the descent to Bealach nan Corp although it improves as it drops through Stank Glen. A final section of minor road leads back to the start.

Ben Ledi
Although there are bigger mountains within the National Park there aren't many as popular as Ben Ledi, and with good reason. This route is a Scottish classic, with good paths, marvellous panoramas and a secluded glen all combining for a superb walk. It's thought that Ben Ledi translates as *Hill of God*, due to the pagan festivals that used to take place on the summit. However it's more likely to mean *Hill of the Slope* (from *Beinn Leitir*), which probably relates to Ben Ledi's shapely southern incline. The return through quiet Stank Glen adds a nice contrast to the walk.

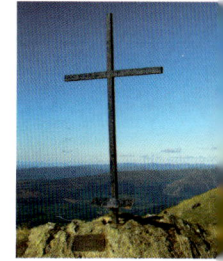

Lawrie Cross on Ben Ledi

Bilberries

The Walk

1. *The walk begins from a car park just off the A84, 3 kilometres west of Kilmahog. Here, leave the A84 onto a road (signed for 'Strathyre Log Cabins') that crosses a bridge over the Garbh Uisge. At its end turn left and follow another narrow road to the car park, which can get very busy, particularly at weekends.*

Walk back along the road, turn left at the **bridge** then bear left onto a path that begins to climb steeply west across open hillside.

In a while the incline eases a little and the craggy eastern slopes of Ben Ledi rise above. Continue to a forestry track.

2. Go straight across onto a path from where a prolonged, steady ascent, through lovely mixed woodland, proceeds along a well-constructed path. When the woodland is left behind, continue on a gradual rise beneath Creag Gorm.

Stunning views open out southeast across Callander to the Ochil Hills and, on a clear day, the Wallace Monument above Stirling.

Walk all the way to the edge of Ben Ledi's southern ridge where

© Crown copyright and/or database right. All rights reserved. Licence number 100047867

Descending Ben Ledi

the path sweeps north. *Below, Loch Venachar is flanked by Ben Gullipen while Tinto Hill, 80 kilometres to the southeast, may well be visible.*

3. As the path heads northwest, on a gradual rise, the gorgeous landscape of The Trossachs and the Southern Highlands opens out, with the panorama becoming even more impressive as the route crosses the domed summit of **Meall Odhar**.

Ben Venue draws the eye towards the mountainous barrier of Ben Lomond and the Arrochar Alps — including The Cobbler's conspicuous outline — while Arran's jagged profile is also striking.

After a short drop, a final stiff rise passes the **Sergeant Harry Lawrie Memorial Cross** to gain the **summit cairn** and **trig**.

The cross commemorates Police Sergeant Harry Lawrie. Harry, who was also the leader of Killin Mountain Rescue, was killed, on the 1st of February 1987, when the RAF helicopter he was travelling in during a rescue operation crashed on Ben More above Crianlarich.

From **Ben Ledi's 879 metre top** *the*

The plains of Stirlingshire and the Sergeant Harry Lawrie Memorial Cross from Ben Ledi

outstanding view extends to Stob Binnein, Ben More, Ben Lawers, Glen Finglas Reservoir and Loch Katrine.

4. From the summit a **marvellous ridge walk** descends northwest then north, with fine views of Lochan nan Corp and Creag na h-Iolaire. The path picks up a **line of fenceposts** at the ridge's highest point, which are followed northwest off the ridge down a grassy/stony path. Approaching **Bealach nan Corp** the ground can be a little wet and muddy.

5. At the base of the bealach turn right onto an initially wet and vague path. It soon becomes more obvious as it descends east into **Stank Glen**.

It is a wonderfully secluded spot with the glen flanked on three sides by steep slopes, and far-reaching views across Stirlingshire.

Eventually the path reaches a stile to the left of a gate. Once across, descend to the base of the glen where the path splits. Keep right and continue through the glen, eventually dropping down to a track just beyond a **small weir**.

6. Bear right onto the track then go round a **barrier** onto a wooded path and descend to a track. Turn right then, after a few metres, just before a **marker post**, go left onto a path.

The path, which can be rough at points,

Useful Information

Loch Lomond and The Trossachs Tourism

Visit Scotland's official website covers everything from accommodation and events to attractions and adventure. **www.visitscotland.com/destinations-maps/loch-lomond-trossachs-forth-valley**

Loch Lomond and The Trossachs National Park

The Loch Lomond and the Trossachs National Park website also has information on things to see and do, plus maps, webcams and news. **www.lochlomond-trossachs.org**

Tourist Information Centres

The main TICs provide free information on everything from accommodation and travel, to what's on and walking advice.

Aberfoyle	01877 381 221	aberfoyle@visitscotland.com
Balloch	01389 753 533	balloch@visitscotland.com
Balmaha	01389 722 100	info@lochlomond-trossachs.org
Callander	01877 330 342	callander@visitscotland.com
Luss	01436 860 229	purdiesofluss@hotmail.co.uk
Tyndrum	01838 400 246	tyndrum@visitscotland.com

Emergencies

Loch Lomond and The Trossachs National Park is covered by the Lomond Mountain Rescue Team (**www.lomondmrt.org.uk**). In a real emergency:

1. Make a note of your location (with OS grid reference, if possible); the name, age and sex of the casualty; their injuries; how many people are in the group; and your mobile phone number.
2. Call 999 or 112 and ask for Police Scotland, and then for Mountain Rescue.
3. Give them your prepared details.
4. Do NOT change position until contacted by the mountain rescue team.

Weather

A three day weather forecast for Loch Lomond and The Trossachs National Park: **www.mwis.org.uk/scottish-forecast/WH**

drops steeply through woodland, high above the **Stank Burn**, soon passing a huge **waterfall** before emerging onto a track. Follow this as it sweeps left then right all the way to a junction.

7. Go right, and continue to a narrow road at the settlement of **Corriechrombie** and follow this back to the start, to complete the walk. ♦

Cruel fate

Bealach nan Corp is part of an old coffin road (it's name means Pass of the Corpses) that ran between Glen Falloch and Balquhidder Kirk. At over 2,000 feet above sea level, the bealach marks the routes highest point. Nearby is Lochan nan Corp, named after a large funeral party — said to contain 200 mourners — who tragically drowned when the frozen surface gave way as they crossed the plateau during winter.